This book should be returned to any branch of the
Lancashire County Library on or before the date shown

2114 CIN

16 SEP 2014

-3 JAN 2015

26 AUG 2015

-7 MAR 2016

Lancashire County Library
Bowran Street
Preston PR1 2UX

Lancashire County Council

www.lancashire.gov.uk/libraries

LL1(A)

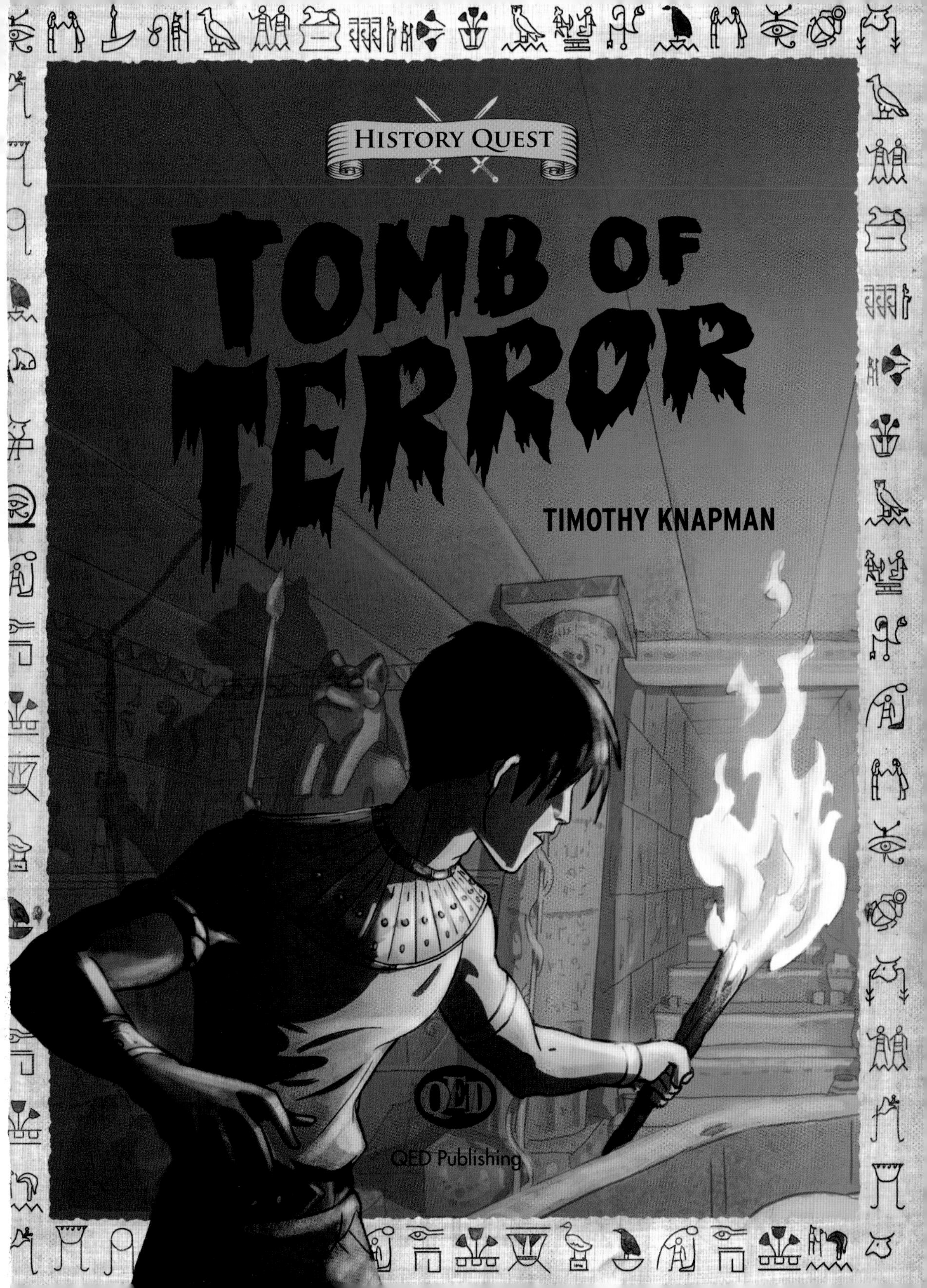
HISTORY QUEST
TOMB OF TERROR
TIMOTHY KNAPMAN
QED
QED Publishing

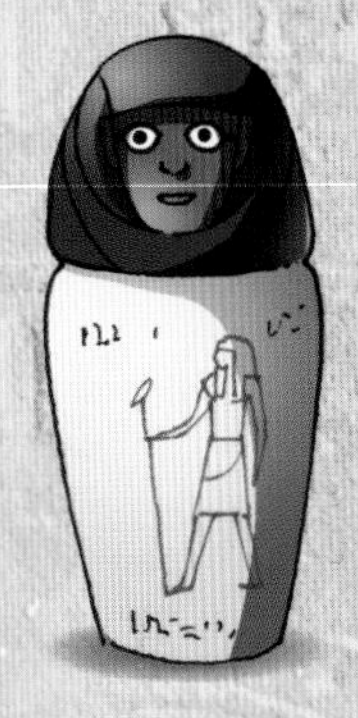
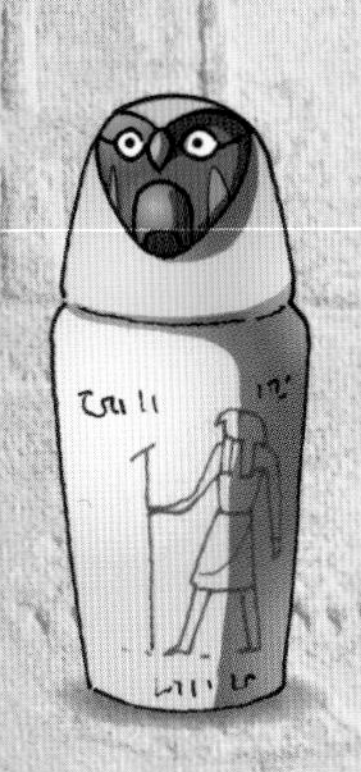
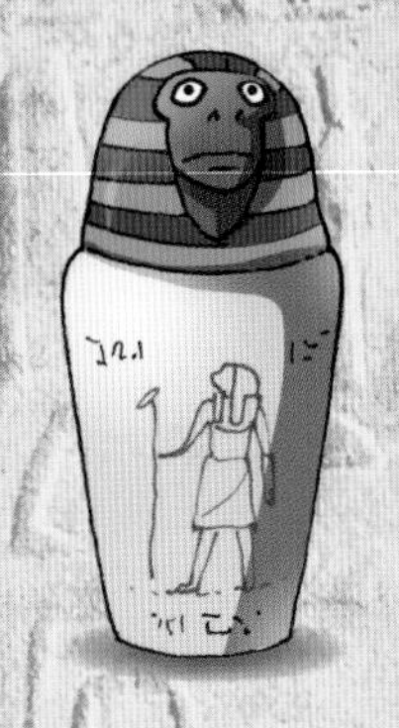

Cover Design: Punch Bowl Design
Illustrator: Andrea Da Rold
Editor: Amanda Askew
Designer: Andrew Crowson

QED Project Editor: Ruth Symons
Managing Editor: Victoria Garrard
Design Manager: Anna Lubecka

Copyright © QED Publishing 2013

First published in the UK in 2013 by
QED Publishing
A Quarto Group company
230 City Road
London EC1V 2TT

www.qed-publishing.co.uk

All rights reserved. No part of this publication may be reproduced, stored in a retrieval system, or transmitted in any form or by any means, electronic, mechanical, photocopying, recording, or otherwise, without the prior permission of the publisher, nor be otherwise circulated in any form of binding or cover other than that in which it is published and without a similar condition being imposed on the subsequent purchaser.

A catalogue record for this book is available from the British Library.

ISBN 978 1 78171 147 7

Printed in China

Picture credits
Shutterstock: Jose Ignacio Soto, 37; PRILL, 41

Lancashire Library Services
30118128080409
PETERS J932KNA
£7.99 15-Nov-2013

How to begin your adventure

Are you ready for an amazing adventure in which you must face deadly foes, survive terrible dangers and solve fiendish puzzles? Then you've come to the right place!

Tomb of Terror isn't an ordinary book – you don't read the pages in order, 1, 2, 3... Instead you jump forwards and backwards through the book as you face a series of challenges. Sometimes you may lose your way, but the story will guide you back to where you need to be. The story begins on page 4, and soon there are questions to answer and puzzles to solve. Each time you choose an answer, you'll see something like this:

IF YOU THINK THE CORRECT ANSWER IS A, GO TO PAGE 37

IF YOU THINK THE CORRECT ANSWER IS B, GO TO PAGE 13 

If you think the correct answer is A, turn to page 37 and look for the same symbol in red. That's where you will find the next part of the story. If you make the wrong choice, the text will explain where you went wrong and let you have another go.

The problems in this book are about life in ancient Egypt. To solve them, you must use your history knowledge, as well as common sense. To help you, there's a glossary of useful words at the back of the book, starting on page 44.

Are you ready?

Turn the page and let your adventure begin!

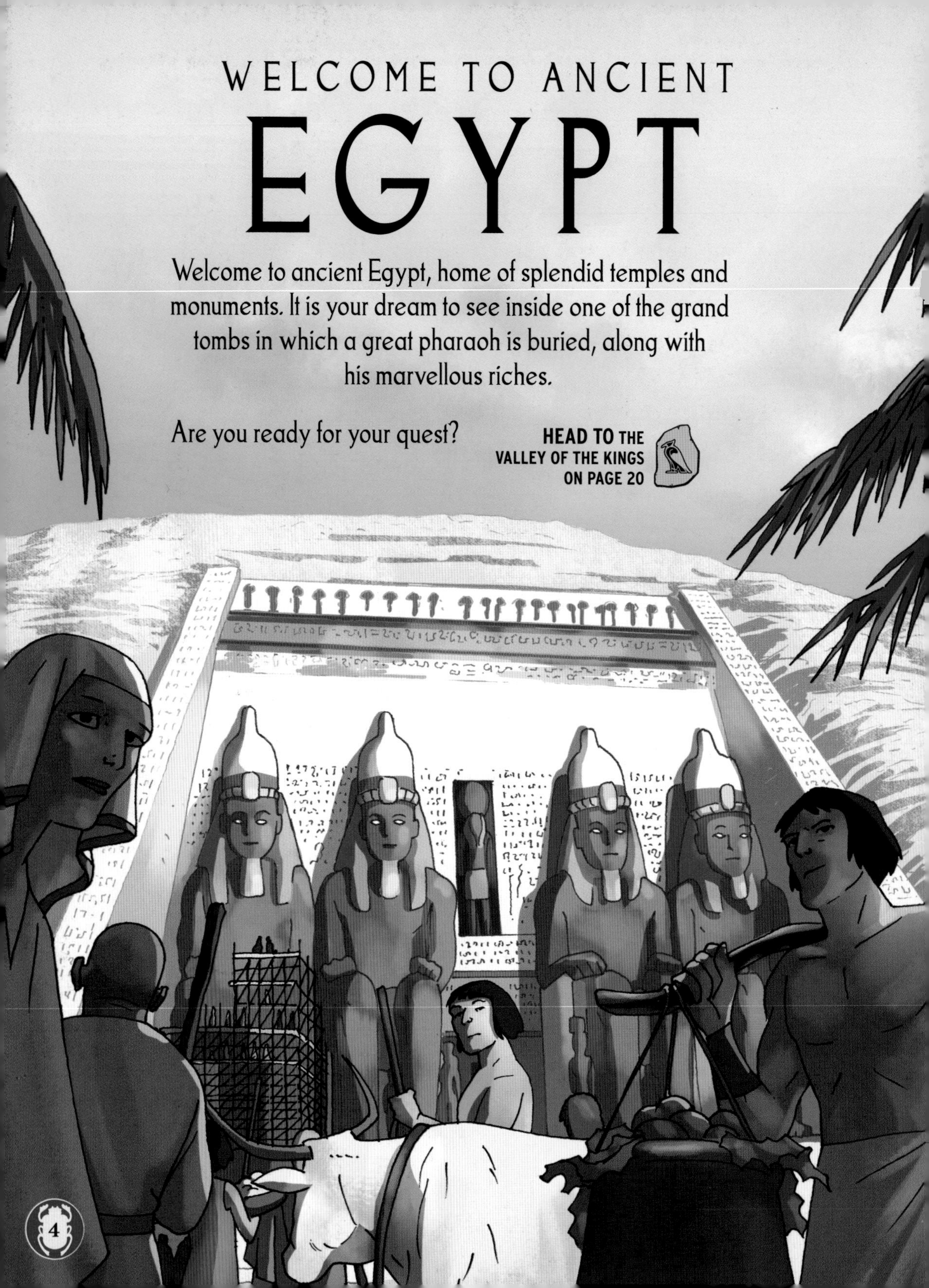

WELCOME TO ANCIENT EGYPT

Welcome to ancient Egypt, home of splendid temples and monuments. It is your dream to see inside one of the grand tombs in which a great pharaoh is buried, along with his marvellous riches.

Are you ready for your quest?

HEAD TO THE VALLEY OF THE KINGS ON PAGE 20

Egyptians used all kinds of make-up, but they didn't paint themselves black.

GO BACK
TO PAGE 19
AND HAVE ANOTHER TRY

Correct! The Nile was very important to the ancient Egyptians. Every year it flooded, making the land good for growing crops.

When you arrive in Memphis, a guard points to a large tent in front of the palace.

TO CREATE THE TREASURES THAT WILL BE PUT INTO THE TOMB?
FLIP TO PAGE 37

TO PRAY FOR THE DEAD PHARAOH?
GO TO PAGE 42

TO MUMMIFY THE DEAD PHARAOH?
TURN TO PAGE 34

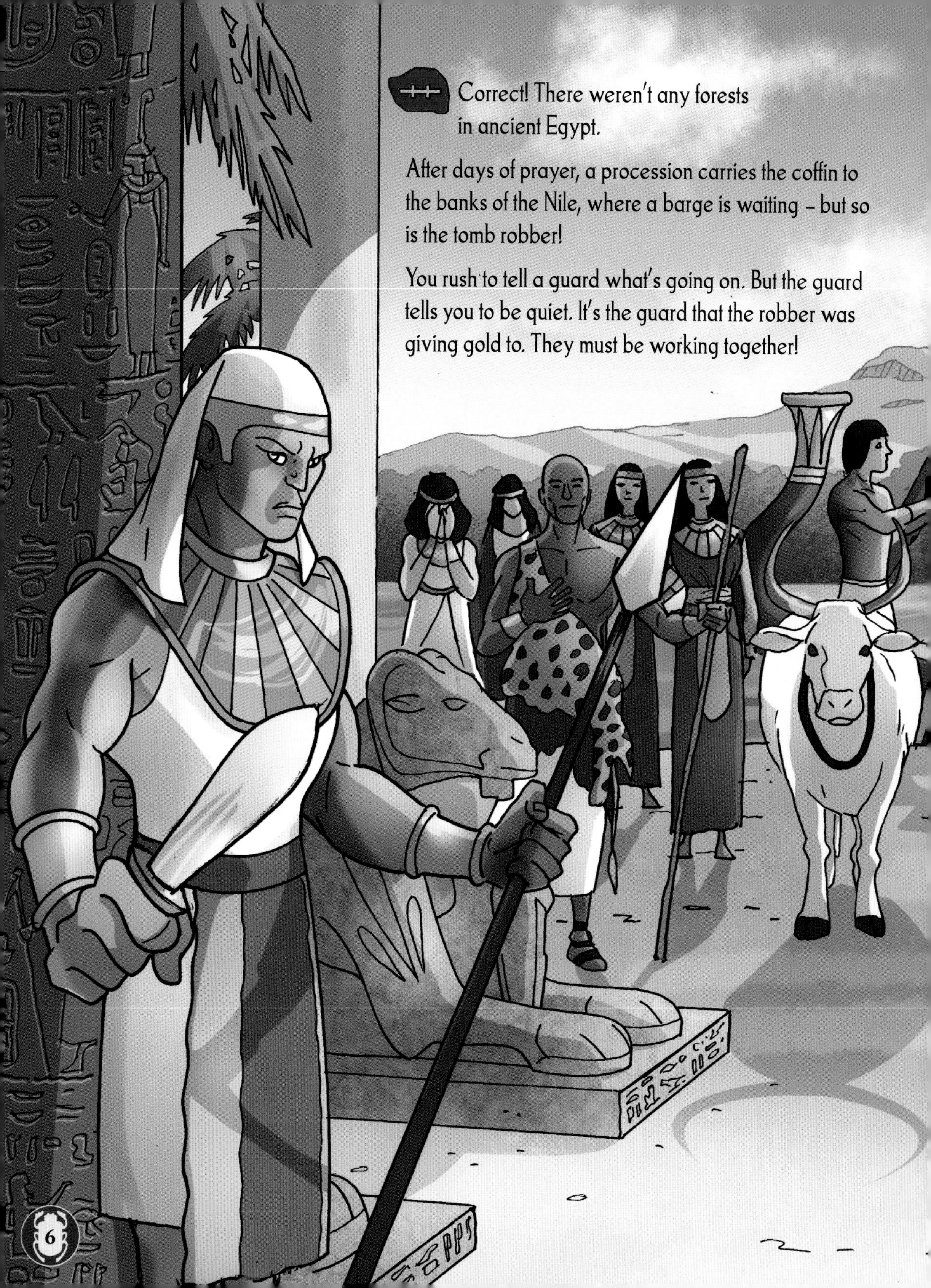

Correct! There weren't any forests in ancient Egypt.

After days of prayer, a procession carries the coffin to the banks of the Nile, where a barge is waiting – but so is the tomb robber!

You rush to tell a guard what's going on. But the guard tells you to be quiet. It's the guard that the robber was giving gold to. They must be working together!

The barge crosses the Nile and reaches the western bank.
Many objects are carried into the tomb – but which will be left outside?
PAPYRUS SCROLLS? GO TO PAGE 21
SMALL FIGURINES OF PEOPLE? TURN TO PAGE 42
FOOD. TURN TO PAGE 36

Pharaohs were great kings, but that's not right.
GO BACK TO PAGE 38 AND THINK AGAIN
The robbers wouldn't destroy the tomb until the treasures were out.
GO BACK TO PAGE 39 AND THINK AGAIN
That's right! Jackals were seen prowling graveyards and so it was a jackal-headed god who oversaw the journey to the underworld.
These are my tools. Which one do I use to remove the brain?
THE SCALPEL? TURN TO PAGE 27
THE HOOK? GO TO PAGE 36
THE TWEEZERS? TURN TO PAGE 43

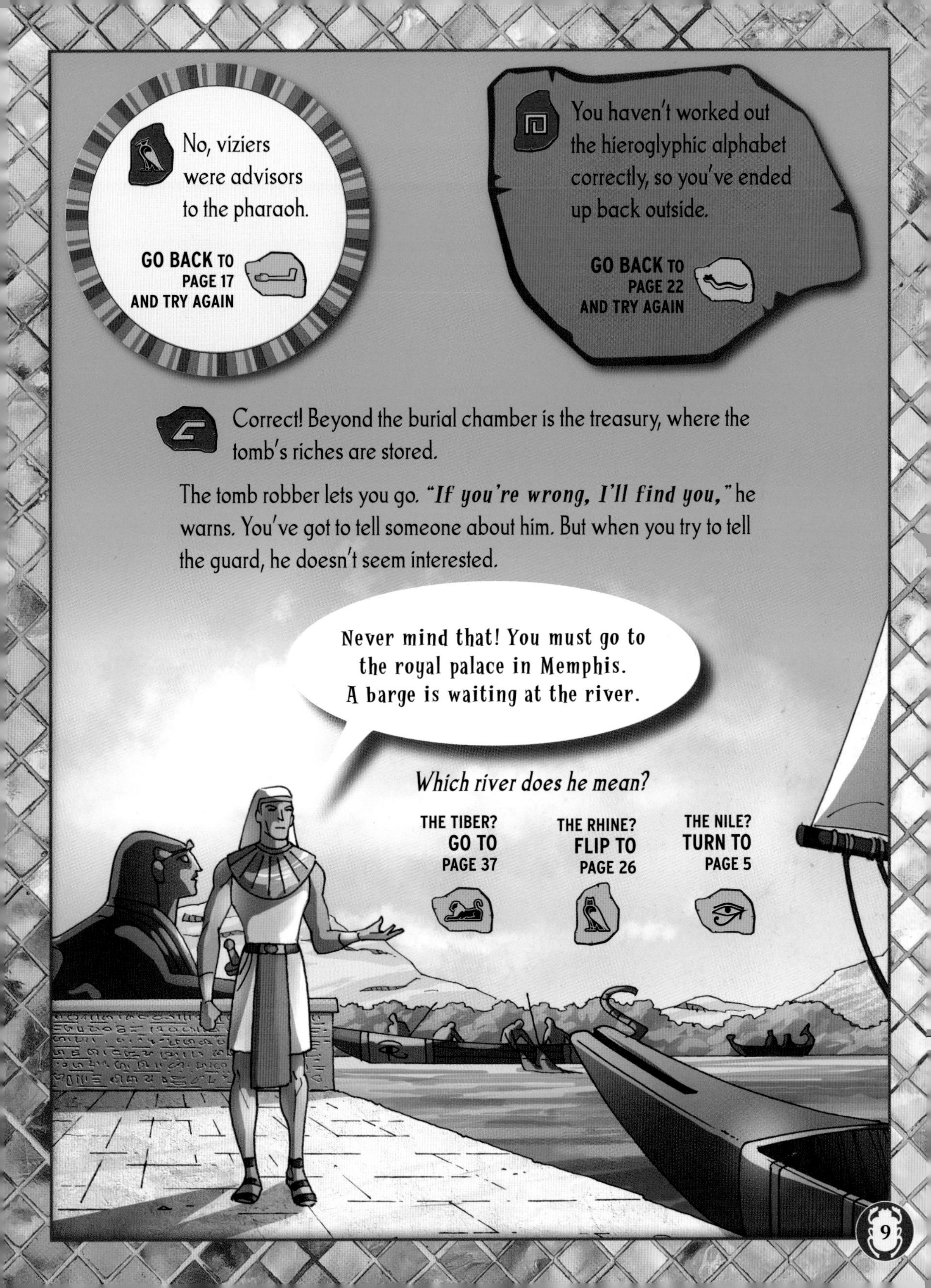
No, viziers were advisors to the pharaoh.
GO BACK TO PAGE 17 AND TRY AGAIN
You haven't worked out the hieroglyphic alphabet correctly, so you've ended up back outside.
GO BACK TO PAGE 22 AND TRY AGAIN
Correct! Beyond the burial chamber is the treasury, where the tomb's riches are stored.
The tomb robber lets you go. "If you're wrong, I'll find you," he warns. You've got to tell someone about him. But when you try to tell the guard, he doesn't seem interested.
Never mind that! You must go to the royal palace in Memphis. A barge is waiting at the river.
Which river does he mean?
THE TIBER? GO TO PAGE 37
THE RHINE? FLIP TO PAGE 26
THE NILE? TURN TO PAGE 5
9

Correct! Cats were very important to the ancient Egyptians, and lots of people kept them as pets. They mummified cats and made statues of them.

You walk over to look at the baskets.

"I will share my lunch with you if you can tell me what these baskets are made of," the woman says.

Think quickly. It's hours since you've eaten. Is it...

PAPYRUS?
TURN TO PAGE 38
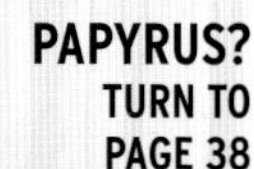

LINEN?
HEAD OVER TO PAGE 13

LEATHER?
GO TO PAGE 31

No, the Ankh symbolizes eternal life.

GO BACK TO PAGE 26 AND CHOOSE AGAIN

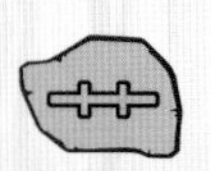

You arrive just in time. The embalmer has already started wrapping the body in bandages.

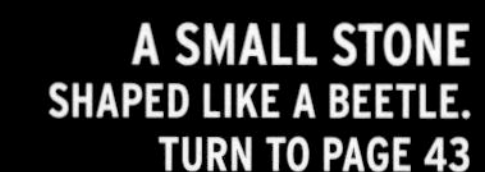

A SMALL STONE SHAPED LIKE A BEETLE.
TURN TO PAGE 43

A DAGGER.
GO TO PAGE 31

A STATUE OF A LION.
FLIP TO PAGE 20
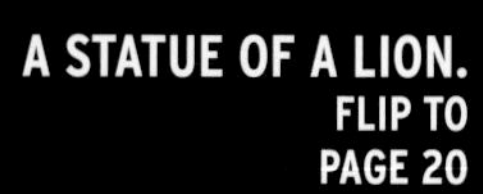
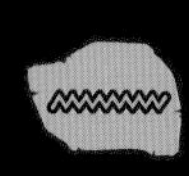

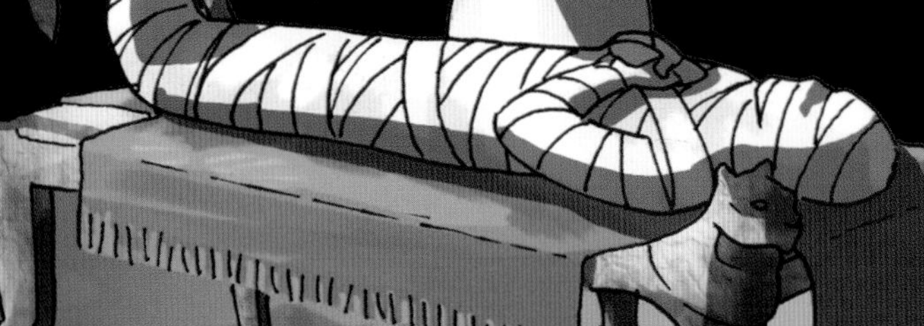

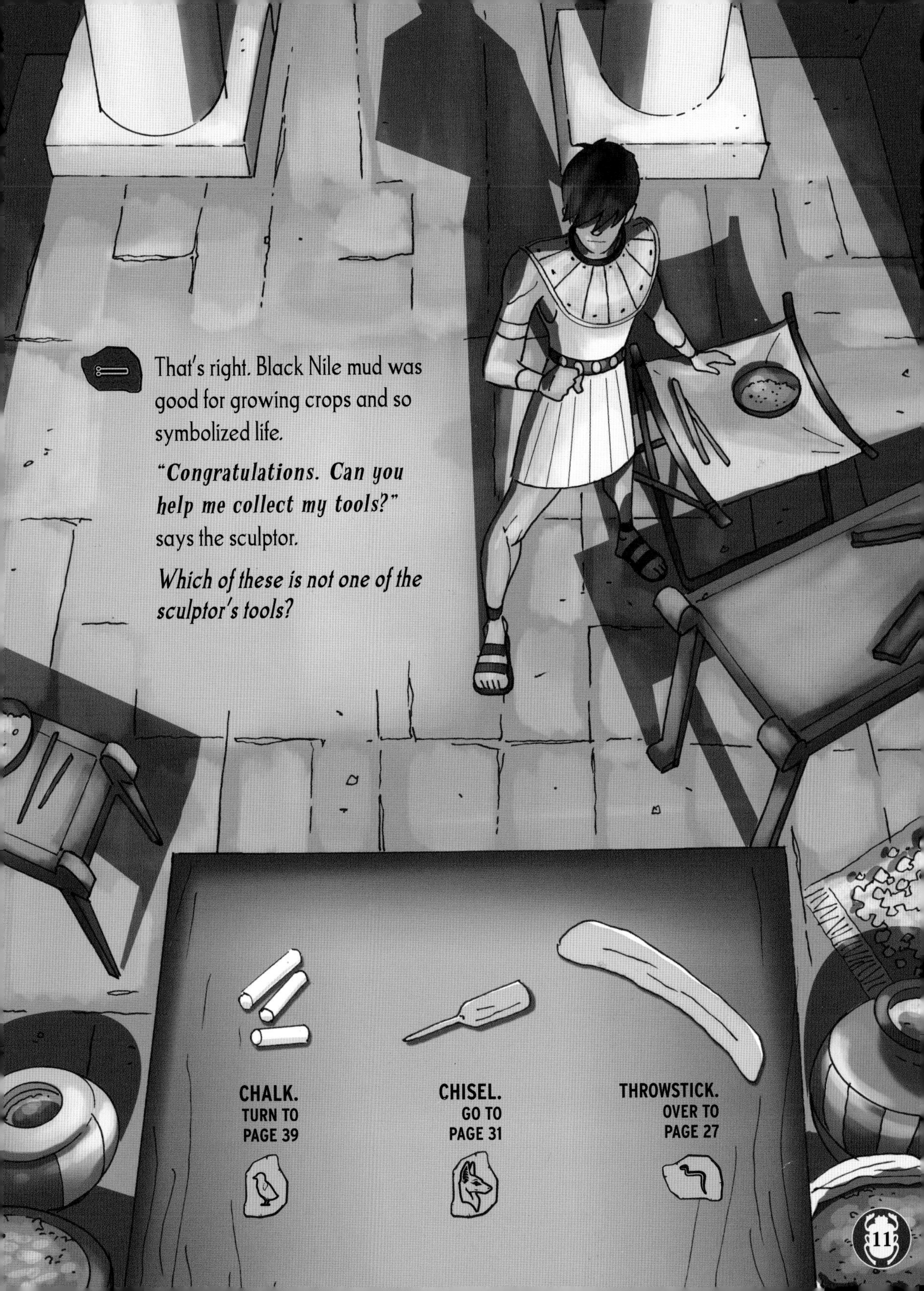
That's right. Black Nile mud was good for growing crops and so symbolized life.
"Congratulations. Can you help me collect my tools?" says the sculptor.
Which of these is not one of the sculptor's tools?
CHALK.
TURN TO PAGE 39
CHISEL.
GO TO PAGE 31
THROWSTICK.
OVER TO PAGE 27

Yes, paper was made from pressed and woven papyrus. It was expensive because it took so long to make.

The woman offers you a piece of bread. You take a big bite – but pain shoots through your teeth!

"Haven't you ever had bread before? You'll get used to the rough texture. Can you guess what causes it?"

SMALL PIECES OF WOOD ARE ADDED TO HELP IT COOK. GO TO PAGE 37

IT'S BAKED TWICE. FLIP TO PAGE 26

THERE'S GRIT IN IT. TURN TO PAGE 41

No, wood wasn't seen as sacred. There was a much more obvious reason.

GO BACK TO PAGE 43 AND TRY AGAIN

That's right – pharaoh was once the name for the king's palace, but in time the name was used for the king himself.

The craftsman is still looking at you suspiciously.

Question three: What does the goddess Bastet have the head of?

A CAT? GO TO PAGE 23

A RAM? TURN TO PAGE 19

A COW? FLIP TO PAGE 41

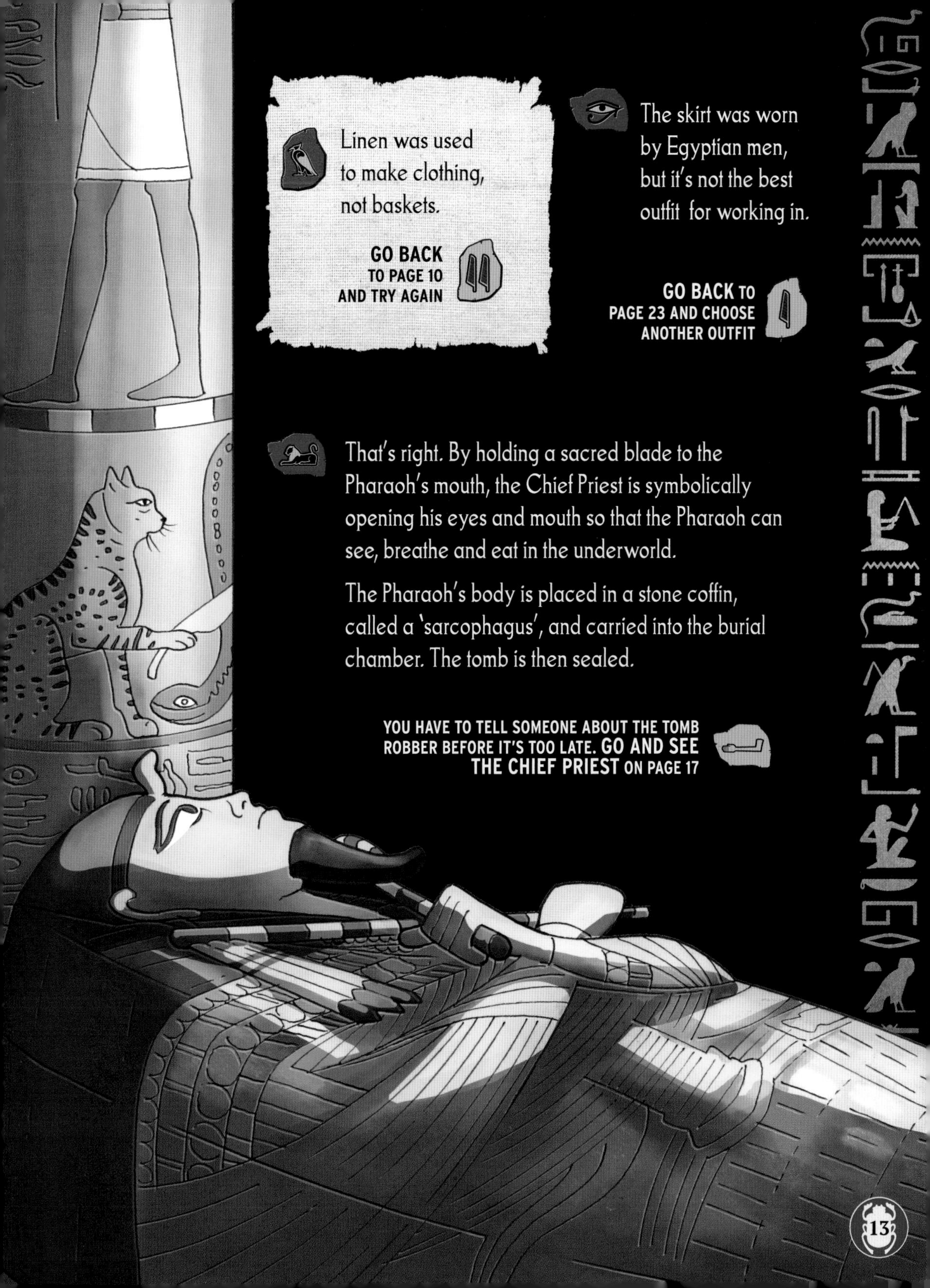

Linen was used to make clothing, not baskets.

GO BACK TO PAGE 10 AND TRY AGAIN

The skirt was worn by Egyptian men, but it's not the best outfit for working in.

GO BACK TO PAGE 23 AND CHOOSE ANOTHER OUTFIT

That's right. By holding a sacred blade to the Pharaoh's mouth, the Chief Priest is symbolically opening his eyes and mouth so that the Pharaoh can see, breathe and eat in the underworld.

The Pharaoh's body is placed in a stone coffin, called a 'sarcophagus', and carried into the burial chamber. The tomb is then sealed.

YOU HAVE TO TELL SOMEONE ABOUT THE TOMB ROBBER BEFORE IT'S TOO LATE. **GO AND SEE THE CHIEF PRIEST** ON PAGE 17

Snakes and scorpions live
in the cool, dark caves.
One bite or sting and
you could be history...
Be careful!
You tumble into a cave and
bump into a large man.
Get back to work with the
other junior artists!
There are three groups of people
painting. Which group are the
junior artists?
GROUP ONE.
GO TO
PAGE 42

GROUP TWO.
TURN TO
PAGE 26
GROUP THREE.
HEAD OVER TO
PAGE 33

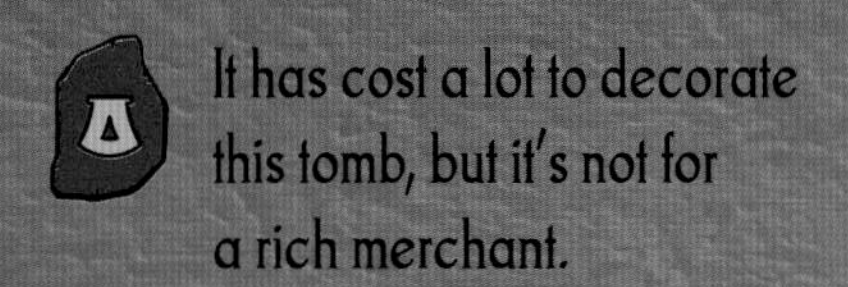

It has cost a lot to decorate this tomb, but it's not for a rich merchant.

GO BACK TO PAGE 42 AND THINK AGAIN

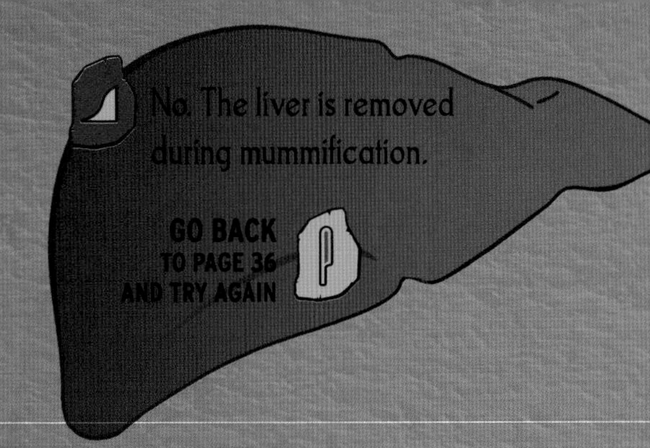

No. The liver is removed during mummification.

GO BACK TO PAGE 36 AND TRY AGAIN

CLUE

Here's the hieroglyphic alphabet to help you answer the question on page 22.

AEO	A	B	C S	C K	D
E Y	F V	G J	G	H	I Y Y
L	M	N	OUW	H	I Y Y
R	S Z	SH	T	U	X

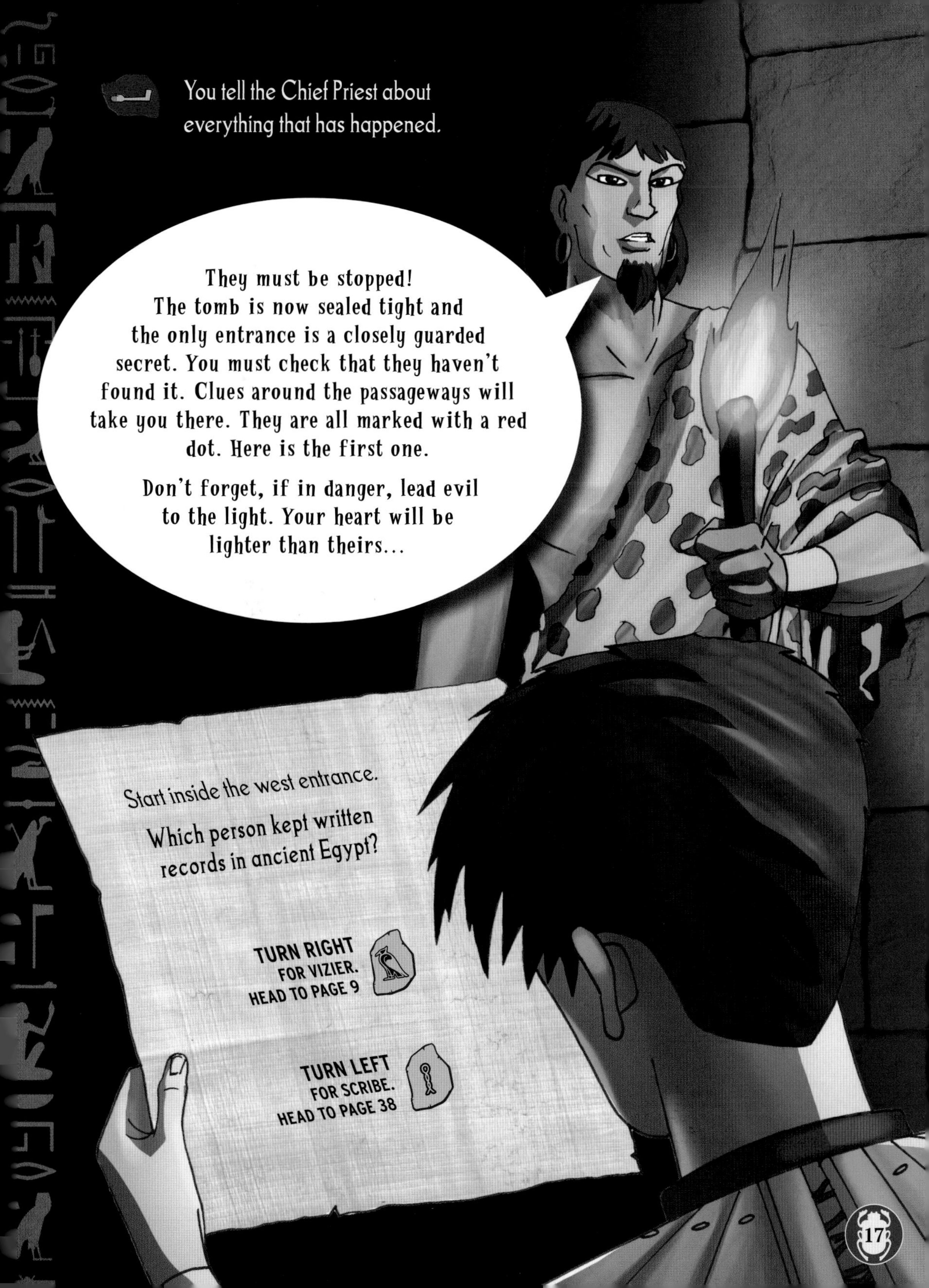
You tell the Chief Priest about everything that has happened.
They must be stopped! The tomb is now sealed tight and the only entrance is a closely guarded secret. You must check that they haven't found it. Clues around the passageways will take you there. They are all marked with a red dot. Here is the first one.
Don't forget, if in danger, lead evil to the light. Your heart will be lighter than theirs...
Start inside the west entrance.
Which person kept written records in ancient Egypt?
TURN RIGHT FOR VIZIER. HEAD TO PAGE 9
TURN LEFT FOR SCRIBE. HEAD TO PAGE 38

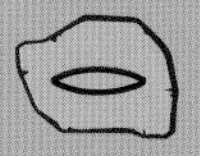

The jackal protects the stomach.

GO BACK
TO PAGE 21
AND PICK
ANOTHER

No, Osiris was not the god of hunting, so he didn't need a bow and arrows.

GO BACK TO
PAGE 32
AND TRY AGAIN

Yes, because fire will melt the gold in the tomb. When the fire is out, the robbers will come back and collect the lumps of cooled gold.

"**Stop!**" you shout. The tomb robbers turn towards you. The Chief Priest told you to lead them to the light. Did he mean outside? You grab a flaming torch to use as a weapon, but you suddenly feel yourself falling.

GO TO PAGE 28
TO FIND OUT
WHAT'S HAPPENING...

No, Khnum, a creator god, had the head of a ram.
GO BACK TO PAGE 12 AND TRY AGAIN
No, the Ba is the symbol of the soul, and does not offer protection.
GO BACK TO PAGE 26 AND TRY AGAIN
That's right. Hapi protects the lungs.
You fill the body with spices and then place it in a mixture of chemicals to dry it out. The embalmer dismisses you. It will be 40 days before the body is ready to be wrapped in bandages.
Back at the tomb, you help the other workers to move a heavy statue of a black-skinned guard into the chamber.
The sculptor beams proudly at his work. "If anyone can tell me why this statue has black skin, you will be rewarded."
Is it...
BECAUSE BLACK WAS THE COLOUR OF NILE MUD, WHICH SYMBOLIZED LIFE? TURN TO PAGE 11
BECAUSE GUARDS PAINTED THEIR SKIN BLACK TO MAKE THEM LOOK STRONG? FLIP TO PAGE 5
19

Statues were placed in the tomb, but they were too large to be wrapped with the mummy.

GO BACK TO PAGE 10 AND HAVE ANOTHER GO

She has shaved off her eyebrows because she's in mourning, but it's not for her husband.

GO BACK TO PAGE 27 AND HAVE ANOTHER TRY

You find yourself in a dry riverbed called the Valley of the Kings. You notice something on the side of the valley and climb up to investigate. It looks like a small entrance, and you squeeze through.

But beware! You've heard terrible stories about the dangers lurking inside tombs.

But what is the worst danger facing you?

THE CURSE OF THE PHARAOH?
GO TO PAGE 36

SNAKES AND SCORPIONS?
GO TO PAGE 14

Cracked it! The heart remains in the body – it will be part of an important ceremony in the afterlife.

The other organs are removed.

"Right, we need to put the organs into the canopic jars to preserve them. Bring me the jar for the lungs."

Each jar has the head of a god to protect the organ inside. Which do you choose?

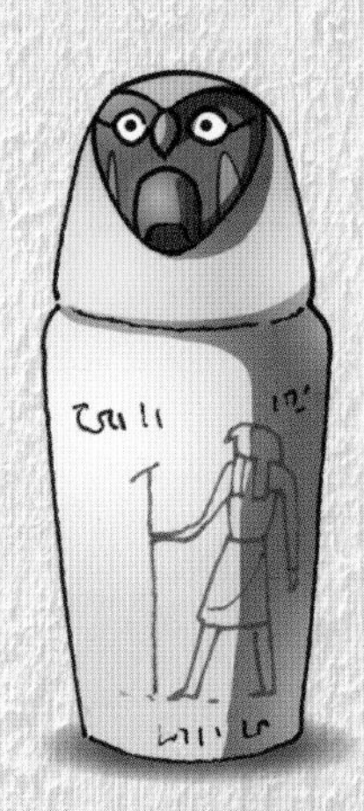

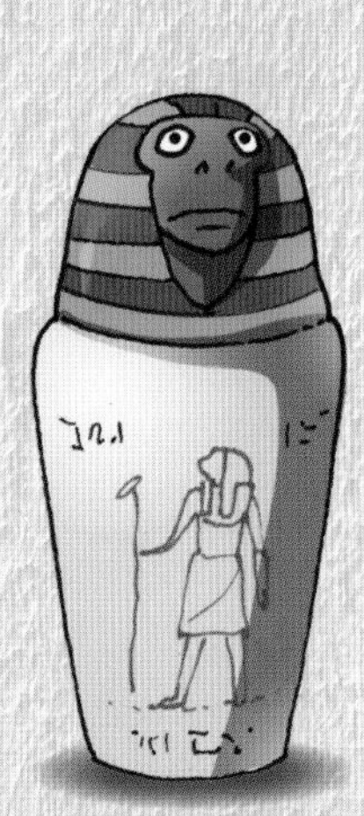

THE MAN IMSETY?
TURN TO PAGE 31

THE FALCON QEBEHSENUEF?
FLIP TO PAGE 37

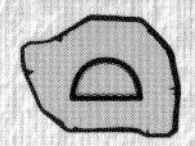

THE BABOON HAPI?
CHECK ON PAGE 19

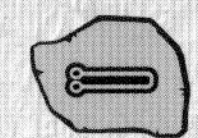

THE JACKAL DUAMUTEF?
GO TO PAGE 18

The scrolls make up a Book of the Dead – a collection of spells to protect the dead person on the journey to the afterlife – so they should be buried in the tomb.

GO BACK TO PAGE 7
AND TRY AGAIN

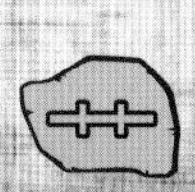

Correct! The Great Pyramid was built in Giza for King Khufu.

At the end of the corridor there are two staircases leading down. Your next clue is written in code, using hieroglyphics. Solve the code and you'll know which way to go.

For a clue, turn to page 16.

Do you?

GO LEFT. GO TO PAGE 39

GO RIGHT. GO TO PAGE 9

No, the coffin is now sealed.

GO BACK TO PAGE 36 AND TRY AGAIN

No, C is the antechamber, where the less valuable goods – such as tables and a chariot – are stored.

GO BACK TO **PAGE 40 AND TRY AGAIN**

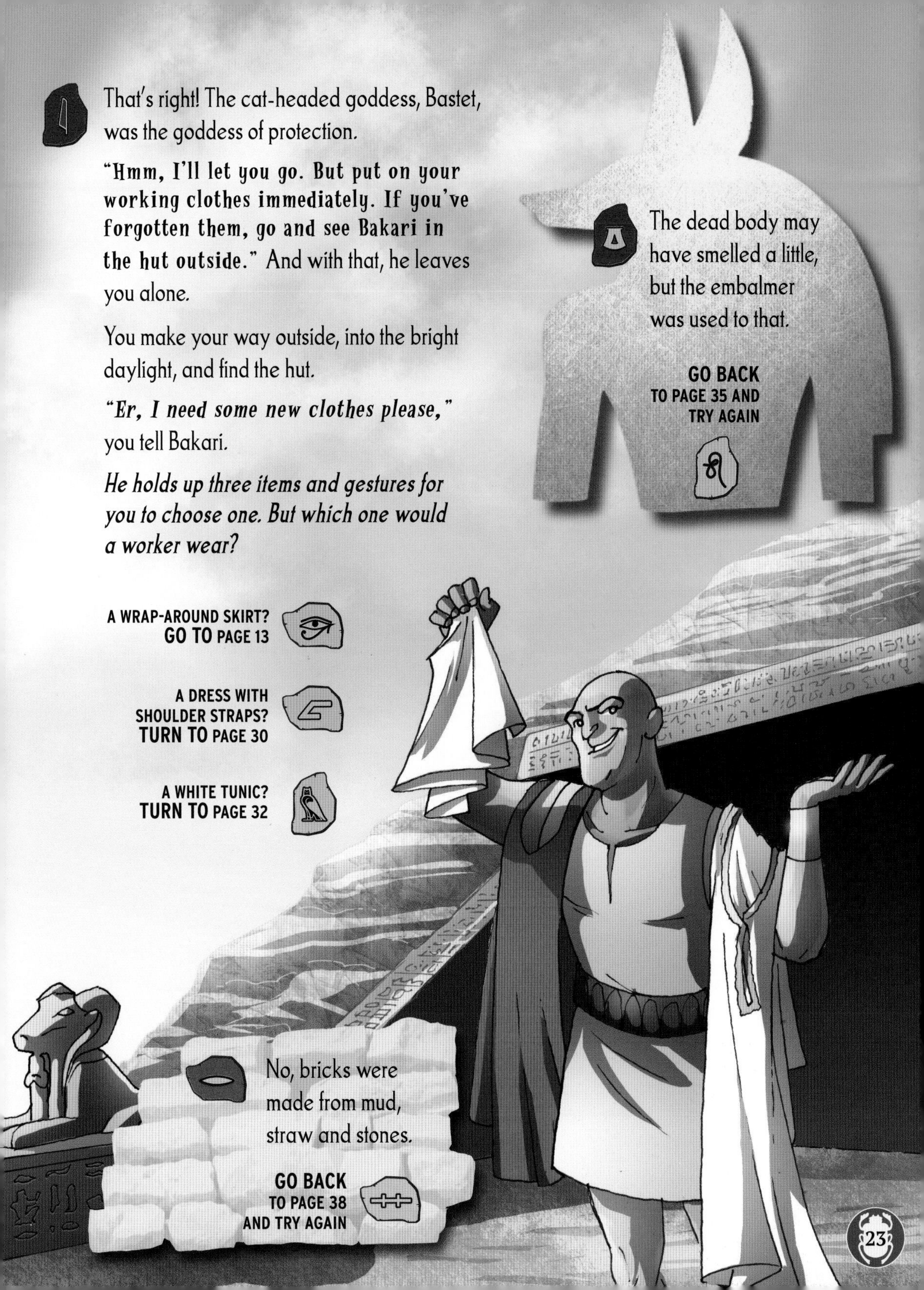

That's right! The cat-headed goddess, Bastet, was the goddess of protection.

"Hmm, I'll let you go. But put on your working clothes immediately. If you've forgotten them, go and see Bakari in the hut outside." And with that, he leaves you alone.

You make your way outside, into the bright daylight, and find the hut.

"Er, I need some new clothes please," you tell Bakari.

He holds up three items and gestures for you to choose one. But which one would a worker wear?

A WRAP-AROUND SKIRT?
GO TO PAGE 13

A DRESS WITH SHOULDER STRAPS?
TURN TO PAGE 30

A WHITE TUNIC?
TURN TO PAGE 32

The dead body may have smelled a little, but the embalmer was used to that.

GO BACK
TO PAGE 35 AND TRY AGAIN

No, bricks were made from mud, straw and stones.

GO BACK
TO PAGE 38
AND TRY AGAIN

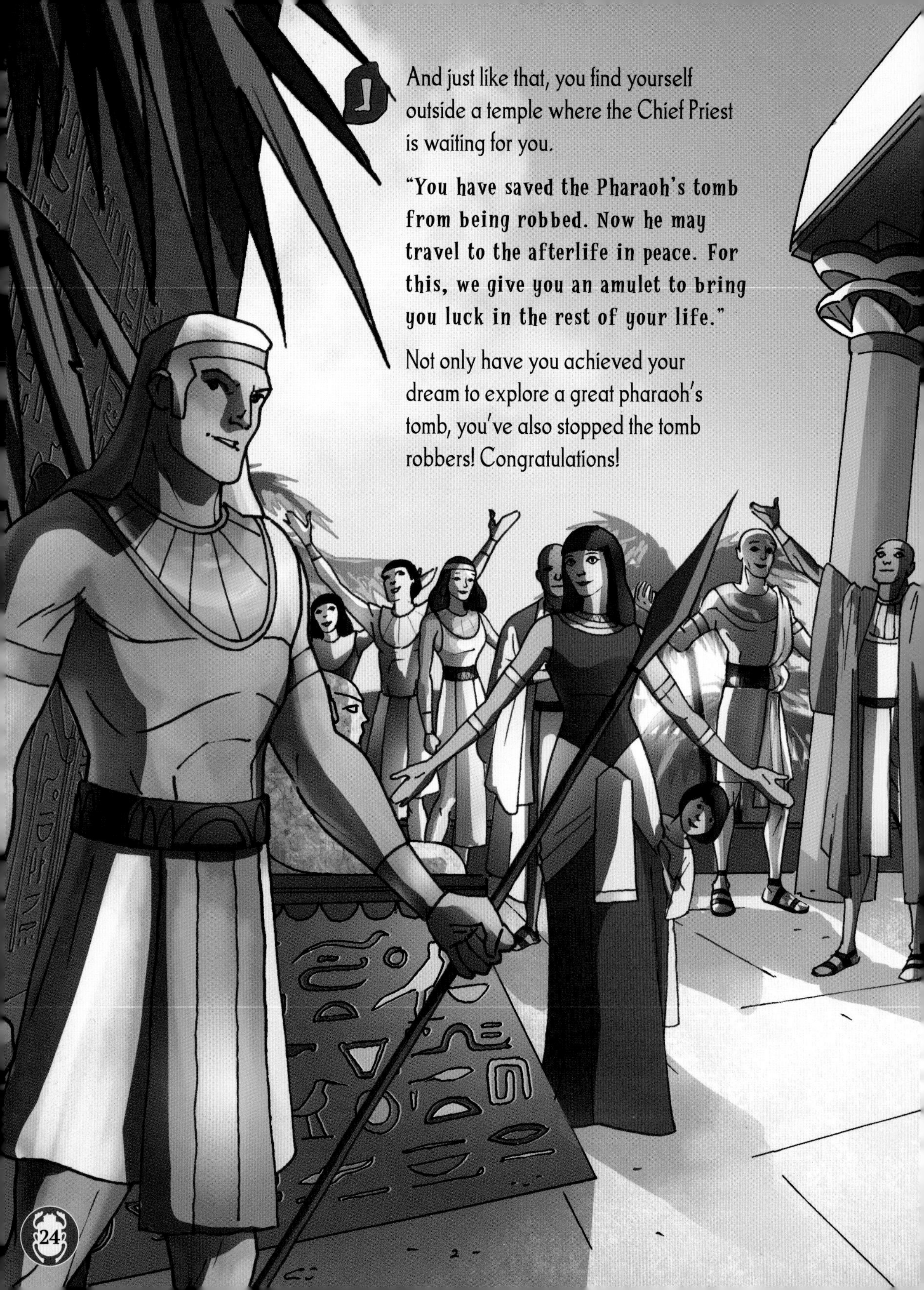
And just like that, you find yourself
outside a temple where the Chief Priest
is waiting for you.
"You have saved the Pharaoh's tomb
from being robbed. Now he may
travel to the afterlife in peace. For
this, we give you an amulet to bring
you luck in the rest of your life."
Not only have you achieved your
dream to explore a great pharaoh's
tomb, you've also stopped the tomb
robbers! Congratulations!

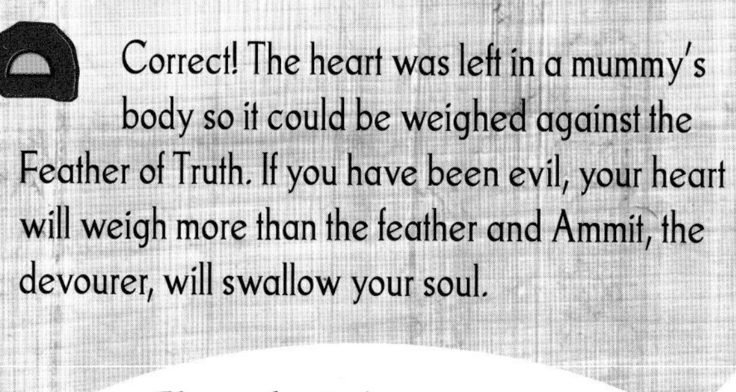

Correct! The heart was left in a mummy's body so it could be weighed against the Feather of Truth. If you have been evil, your heart will weigh more than the feather and Ammit, the devourer, will swallow your soul.

The scales balance – your heart has passed the test. Our magic will now return your heart to your body. Normally you would pass to the afterlife, but it is not your time yet... Just choose the symbol of protection, and you can go back to the mortal world.

Which symbol do you choose?

THE EYE OF HORUS. **HEAD TO PAGE 30**

THE ANKH. **GO TO PAGE 10**

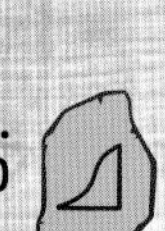

THE BA. **YOU'RE TRANSPORTED TO PAGE 19**

No, the Rhine is in Germany!

GO BACK TO PAGE 9 AND TRY AGAIN

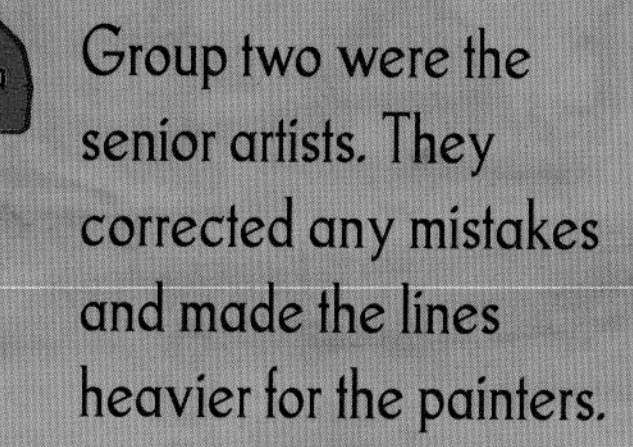

Group two were the senior artists. They corrected any mistakes and made the lines heavier for the painters.

GO BACK TO PAGE 14 AND TRY AGAIN

The bread would be burned if it were baked twice.

GO BACK TO PAGE 12 AND TRY AGAIN

The scalpel is for cutting into the body, not removing the brain.

GO BACK
TO PAGE 8
AND CHOOSE ANOTHER TOOL

Pharaohs were thought to be sons of the sun-god Re, but that's not right.

GO BACK TO
PAGE 38
AND THINK AGAIN

A throwstick isn't a tool. It was used by the Egyptians for hunting birds.

"**Thank you,**" says the sculptor. "**I'll meet you outside in a few minutes.**"

Outside, a group of women are making baskets. You notice that one of them has shaved off her eyebrows.

Why would she do this?

IT'S FASHIONABLE.
GO TO PAGE 37

SHE'S IN MOURNING
FOR HER HUSBAND.
FLIP TO PAGE 20

SHE'S IN MOURNING
FOR HER CAT.
TURN TO PAGE 10

You land hard on the ground. You look around – it looks like paintings you've seen of the underworld! The torch must have transported you there!

You see a great hall ahead of you and head towards it. The gods Anubis, Thoth and Osiris are waiting for you.

Before you may pass, we must weigh one of your organs against the Feather of Truth. But which one?
CLUE: It's the one organ left in the body during mummification.
THE HEART? FLIP TO PAGE 26
THE LUNGS? TURN TO PAGE 37

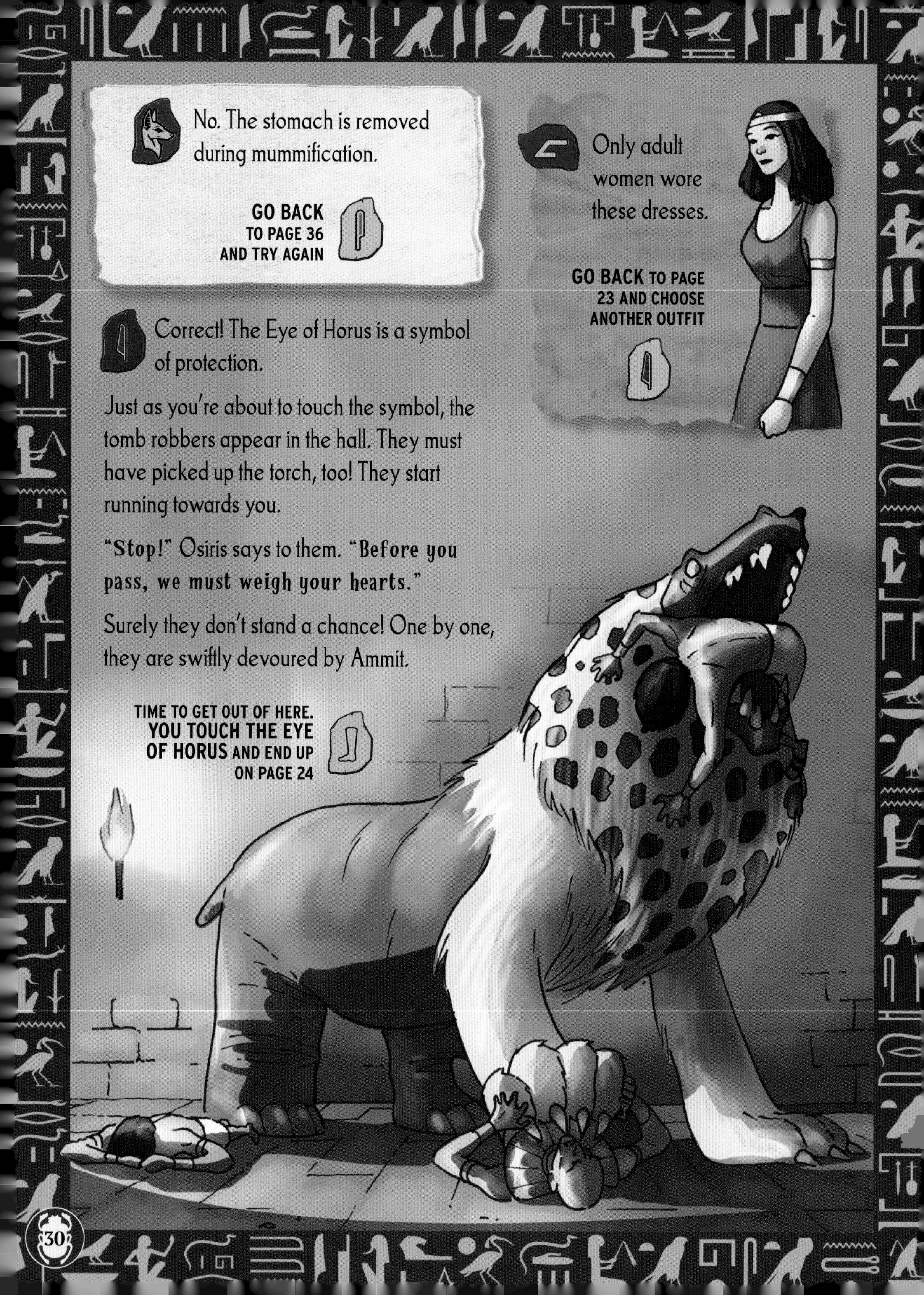
No. The stomach is removed during mummification.
GO BACK TO PAGE 36 AND TRY AGAIN
Only adult women wore these dresses.
GO BACK TO PAGE 23 AND CHOOSE ANOTHER OUTFIT
Correct! The Eye of Horus is a symbol of protection.
Just as you're about to touch the symbol, the tomb robbers appear in the hall. They must have picked up the torch, too! They start running towards you.
"Stop!" Osiris says to them. "Before you pass, we must weigh your hearts."
Surely they don't stand a chance! One by one, they are swiftly devoured by Ammit.
TIME TO GET OUT OF HERE. YOU TOUCH THE EYE OF HORUS AND END UP ON PAGE 24

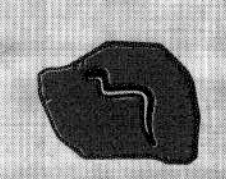

No, Osiris was not the god of music.

GO BACK
TO PAGE 32
AND TRY AGAIN

No, the man jar contains the liver.

GO BACK
TO PAGE 21
AND CHOOSE AGAIN

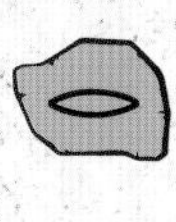

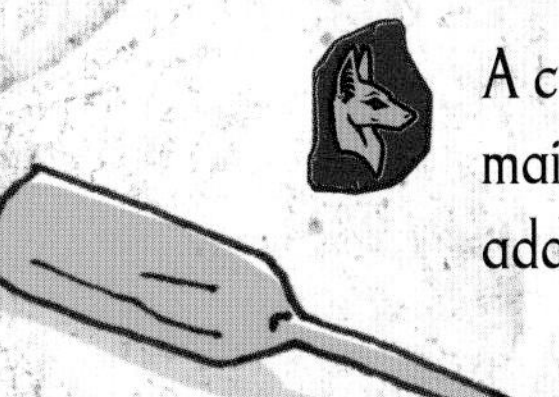

A chisel was a sculptor's main tool! It was used to add fine detail to a statue.

GO BACK
TO PAGE 11
AND TRY AGAIN

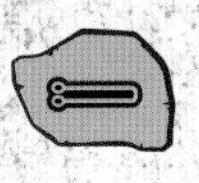

A dagger isn't enough to protect the mummy from evil in the afterlife.

GO BACK
TO PAGE 10
AND THINK AGAIN

The walls are covered with pictures of gods, but it's not the tomb of a priest.

GO BACK
TO PAGE 42
AND HAVE ANOTHER GO

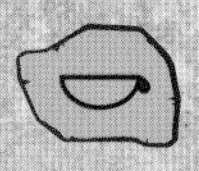

No, leather was rarely used in Egypt.

GO BACK
TO PAGE 10
AND TRY AGAIN

Good choice. The white tunic will protect you from the sun's heat.

But you've got no gold to pay Bakari!

What should the god Osiris be holding?

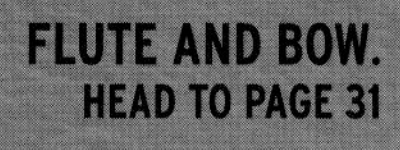

FLUTE AND BOW.
HEAD TO PAGE 31

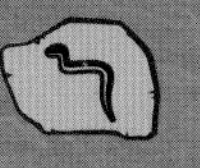

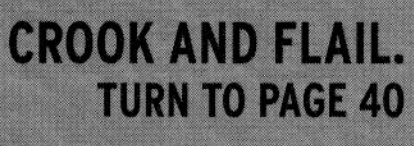

CROOK AND FLAIL.
TURN TO PAGE 40

BOW AND ARROWS.
GO TO PAGE 18

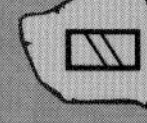

You wake up in a strange room with a woman leaning over you.
You were brought here after eating poisoned honey. You've been asleep for 40 days.
No, group three were the painters. Tomb paintings often showed the dead person in young life, having fun. The ancient Egyptians believed that these scenes would come to life in the next world.
GO BACK TO PAGE 14 AND TRY AGAIN
The mummification! The funeral! Have I missed them?
No, they're happening today.
YOU DASH OUT AND RACE TO THE BEAUTIFUL HOUSE ON PAGE 10

That's right! This is where the Pharaoh's body will be mummified.
Inside the Beautiful House is a long table with the dead Pharaoh on it, lots of jars and a tray full of instruments.

It's about time you got here. Mummification is a long process and we need to get started. You're new so you've got a lot to learn about the rituals involved. Do you know why I wear this mask?
TO REPRESENT ANUBIS, THE GOD OF THE UNDERWORLD. TURN TO PAGE 8
THE DEAD BODY SMELLS BAD. TURN TO PAGE 23
TO HIDE HIS IDENTITY. GO TO PAGE 39

Well done! The brain was removed using a hook. It was not thought to be important, so was thrown away.

I will now remove all the organs, except one. Do you know which one?

THE LIVER.
GO TO PAGE 16

THE HEART.
FLIP TO PAGE 21

THE STOMACH.
TURN TO PAGE 30

That's just a story! When the Pharaoh Tutankhamun's tomb was opened in 1922, some workers died shortly afterwards. It was said that the Pharaoh had cursed them for disturbing his rest. However, many other people involved – including archaeologist Howard Carter – lived to a great age.

GO BACK TO PAGE 20 AND TRY AGAIN

Correct! Food was offered to the Pharaoh, but on special offering tables outside the tomb.

The tomb robber is getting impatient. "**This is taking too long. What are they doing now?**"

The Pharaoh's coffin is stood upright, and the Chief Priest holds a blade to its mouth.

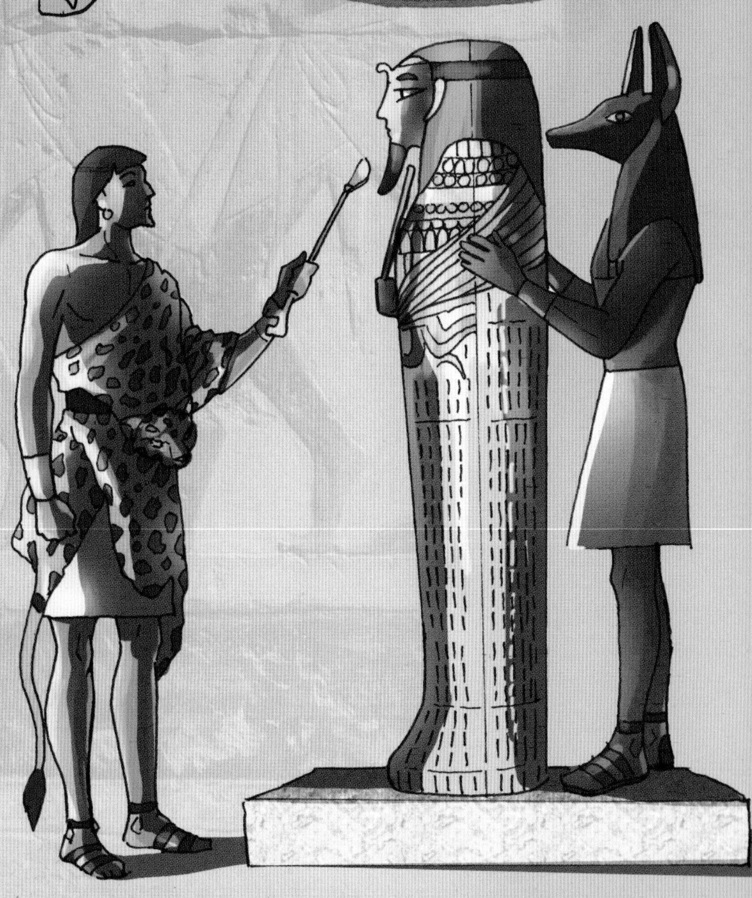

HE IS GOING TO CUT A HOLE IN THE COFFIN.
TURN TO PAGE 22

HE IS PERFORMING THE OPENING OF THE MOUTH CEREMONY.
GO TO PAGE 13

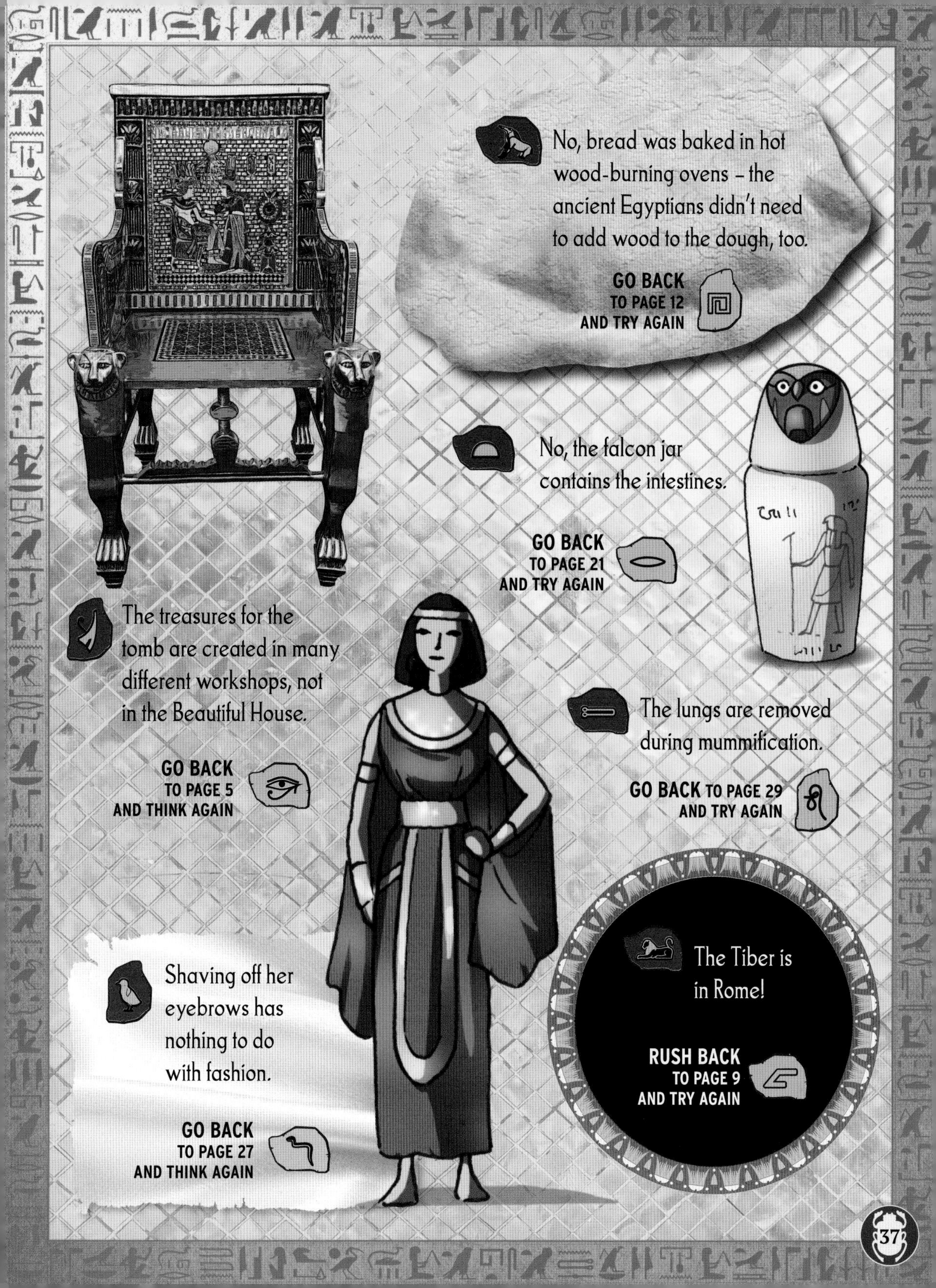

No, bread was baked in hot wood-burning ovens – the ancient Egyptians didn't need to add wood to the dough, too.

GO BACK TO PAGE 12 AND TRY AGAIN

No, the falcon jar contains the intestines.

GO BACK TO PAGE 21 AND TRY AGAIN

The treasures for the tomb are created in many different workshops, not in the Beautiful House.

GO BACK TO PAGE 5 AND THINK AGAIN

The lungs are removed during mummification.

GO BACK TO PAGE 29 AND TRY AGAIN

The Tiber is in Rome!

RUSH BACK TO PAGE 9 AND TRY AGAIN

Shaving off her eyebrows has nothing to do with fashion.

GO BACK TO PAGE 27 AND THINK AGAIN

Yes, baskets were often made of papyrus reeds or palm leaves.

"We also make something precious from papyrus. Do you know what?"

BRICKS. GO TO PAGE 23

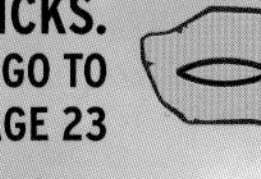

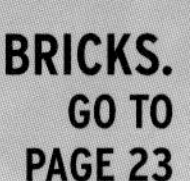

PAPER. TURN TO PAGE 12

Correct. Scribes kept daily records for everything, including which building materials were used and which laws were set.

You walk down the corridor until it splits into two. There's a note on the wall.

Where is the Great Pyramid of Egypt?

ABU SIMBEL. TAKE THE LEFT-HAND CORRIDOR ON PAGE 41

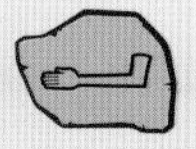

GIZA. TAKE THE RIGHT-HAND CORRIDOR ON PAGE 22

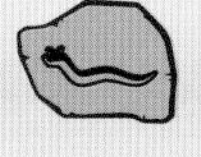

That's right. This is a pharaoh's tomb. But the craftsman sneers.

GREAT KING? TURN TO PAGE 8

GREAT HOUSE? FLIP TO PAGE 12

GREAT GOD? GO STRAIGHT TO PAGE 27

Well done! You take the left staircase, which leads into the tomb. You tiptoe into the chamber. There's light flickering ahead of you and you can hear voices.
"Start the fire," one of them orders.
Why would they do that?
THEY WANT TO DESTROY THE TOMB. GO TO PAGE 8
IT'S EASIER TO STEAL THE GOLD THAT WAY. GO TO PAGE 18
No, the embalmer didn't need to hide his identity.
GO BACK TO PAGE 35 AND TRY AGAIN
Chalk was used to mark out where the sculptor needed to chisel.
GO BACK TO PAGE 11 TO CHOOSE SOMETHING ELSE

That's right. Osiris held a crook and flail to symbolize his kingship. He was god of the afterlife, the underworld and the dead. You take your clothes and head back to the tomb.
On the way, you spot a man offering gold to one of the guards. The guard sees you and shoos the man away.
You enter the tomb and the man follows you inside. You turn around and he's holding a knife.
Show me where the treasury is or I'll cut your throat!
He pushes a plan of the tomb into your hand. You'll have to tell him the truth, but where is the treasury?
A? GO TO PAGE 9
B? FLIP TO PAGE 43
C? TURN TO PAGE 22

No, Abu Simbel is where great temples were built for Ramesses II.

GO BACK TO PAGE 38 AND TRY AGAIN

No, Hathor, the goddess of motherhood, had the head of a cow.

GO BACK TO PAGE 12 AND TRY AGAIN

That's right. The grit came from the stones that were used to grind the flour.

The woman leaves as the sculptor comes over, holding a jar.

"The tomb guard gave me this honey to thank me for my work. I will share it with you as a reward."

You have the first taste. Suddenly you feel your throat tightening and your tongue seems too big for your mouth. Everything goes black.

GO TO PAGE 33 TO FIND OUT WHAT'S HAPPENED TO YOU!

Correct! Group one were the junior artists, who drew the basic outlines of the painting.
When the man isn't looking, you sneak away. But another craftsman stops you.
"I haven't seen you here before!" he snaps. "You will need to answer some questions so I know you're supposed to be here."
Many prayers will be said for the Pharaoh, but not at the Beautiful House.
GO BACK TO PAGE 5 AND THINK AGAIN
Question one: This is the most beautiful tomb we have ever made. So who are we going to bury here?
The small figurines were placed in the tomb to work for the Pharaoh in the afterlife.
GO BACK TO PAGE 7 AND TRY AGAIN.
A RICH MERCHANT? GO TO PAGE 16
A PRIEST? HURRY TO PAGE 31
A PHARAOH? TURN TO PAGE 38

No, B is the burial chamber. There's no room in there for anything except the coffin.

GO BACK TO PAGE 40 AND TRY AGAIN

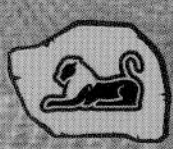

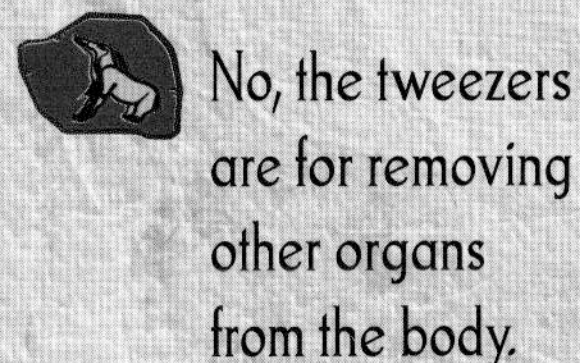

No, the tweezers are for removing other organs from the body.

GO BACK TO PAGE 8 AND TRY AGAIN

That's right! A scarab beetle amulet was placed on the mummy's heart to protect the soul on its journey to the afterlife.

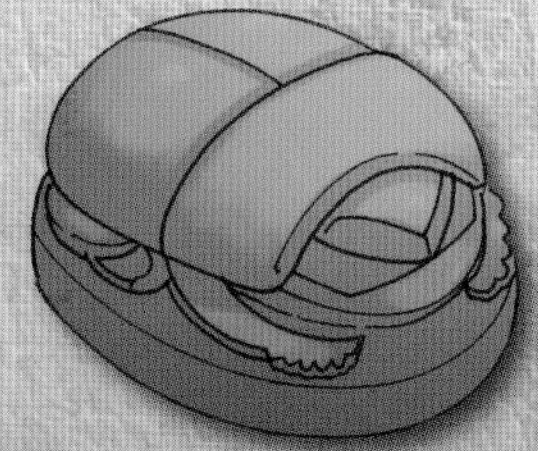

The embalmer puts a gold mask on the Pharaoh's face. Then the Pharaoh's body is placed in a golden coffin.

WOOD WAS SACRED TO THE SUN GOD. GO TO PAGE 12

THERE WERE FEW TREES IN EGYPT, SO WOOD WAS SCARCE. TURN TO PAGE 6

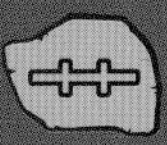

Glossary

Afterlife
Ancient Egyptians believed in life after death. If the person's life had been good, their afterlife would be a heavenly place.

Amulet
An object that can protect its owner from harm, or bring them good luck.

Ankh
A symbol of eternal life. Only kings, queens and gods could carry this symbol because whoever possessed it had power over life and death.

Antechamber
The room in a tomb where less valuable goods were stored.

Ba
The Ba is the nearest the ancient Egyptians came to a modern idea of the soul, and it is often pictured as a bird with a human head.

Beautiful House
The tent where a body was embalmed, or preserved, after death.

Book of the Dead
A collection of spells to protect a dead person on their journey to the afterlife.

Burial chamber
The room in which a mummy was placed within a tomb, along with possessions needed in the afterlife.

Canopic jar
A container for storing important body organs removed during the mummification process.

Chief Priest
The priest who carried out the pharaoh's funeral.

Embalmer
The person who preserved a body after death.

Eye of Horus
A symbol of protection.

Feather of Truth
The ancient Egyptians believed that at the entrance to the underworld a person's heart was weighed against the Feather of Truth. If they had been evil, the heart would weigh more than the feather and Ammit, the devourer, would swallow their soul.

God
Ancient Egyptians worshipped many gods. Each god looked after something. For example, Anubis was the god of the dead.

Hieroglyphics
A form of sacred writing made up of symbolic pictures. It is found on many tombs and sacred monuments.

Memphis
Once the capital of ancient Egypt, Memphis was a great city near the point where the Nile flowed into the Mediterranean Sea.

Merchant
A person who trades goods for other goods or money.

Mummification
The process of preserving a dead body so the soul could move to the afterlife. It could take up to 70 days. First the organs were removed, then the body was soaked in natron (salt) for many days. Finally it was wrapped in bandages.

Nile
The main river flowing through ancient Egypt. The Egyptians depended on it flooding every year to make the soil fertile, so crops could be grown.

Opening of the Mouth ceremony
The Chief Priest held a sacred blade to the mummified pharaoh's mouth, symbolically opening the pharaoh's eyes and mouth so that he could see, breathe and eat in the underworld.

Papyrus
A type of reed used to make paper, baskets and other materials in ancient Egypt.

Pharaoh
A ruler of ancient Egypt. The most famous Pharaoh is Tutankhamun.

Procession
A line of people moving slowly as part of a ceremony.

Pyramid
A massive stone structure with a square base and sloping sides. The pyramids were used as burial places for pharaohs until about 2150 BCE.

Sarcophagus
Made of stone, this was the last of the series of coffins in which a pharaoh's body would be placed.

Scarab beetle
A symbol of good luck or everlasting life.

Temple
A building where people went to worship the gods.

Tomb
A place where dead bodies were buried.

Tunic
Simple garments made of linen that reached the knee. They were worn by both men and women and were usually white.

Tutankhamun
He became Pharaoh at only ten years old and ruled from about 1332 to 1323 BCE. His tomb was found untouched in 1922 CE by archaeologist Howard Carter.

Underworld
Also called the Duat. Ancient Egyptians had to pass through the underworld after death to reach the afterlife. The underworld was ruled by Osiris. It was a terrifying place full of monsters.

Valley of the Kings
From the 16th to the 11th century BCE, the place where tombs for the pharaohs and other powerful Egyptians were built.

Vizier
An advisor to the Pharaoh.

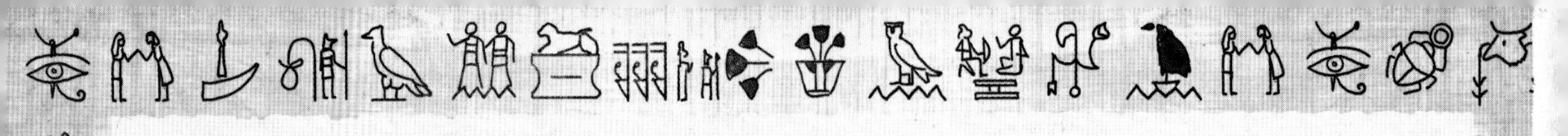

Taking it further

The History Quest books are designed to inspire children to develop and apply their historical knowledge through compelling adventure stories. For each story, children must solve a series of historical problems on their way to completing an exciting quest.

The books do not follow a page-by-page order. The reader jumps forwards and backwards through the book according to the answers given to the problems. If their answers are correct, the reader progresses to the next part of the story; incorrect answers are fully explained before the reader is directed back to attempt the problem once again. Additional help may be found in the glossary at the back of the book.

To support the development of your child's historical knowledge you can:

- Read the book with your child.
- Solve the initial problems and discover how the book works.
- Continue reading with your child until he or she is using the book confidently, following the 'Go to' instructions to the next puzzle or explanation.
- Encourage your child to read on alone. Prompt your child to tell you how the story is developing, and what problems they have solved.
- Point out the differences and similarities of life in ancient Egypt compared with life today – what we wear, eat and do for fun.
- Discuss what it would be like if an ancient Egyptian visited us today. Or if we went back in time to ancient Egypt.
- Take advantage of the many sources of historical information – libraries, museums and documentaries. The Internet is another valuable resource, and there is plenty of material specially aimed at children. Take care only to visit websites endorsed by respected educational authorities, such as museums and universities.
- Remember, we learn most when we're enjoying ourselves, so make history fun!